ACCOUNTING
Dreams & Delusions

Scenes from professional paradise,
and what really happens
in the accounting industry.

KRISTEN RAMPE CPA

Editor Caleb Newquist
Designer Lauren Elaine Coleman
Photography see the back of the book

Caper Artisanal Publishing
38 Fulton Street West, Suite 400
Grand Rapids, Michigan 49503

Printed in the USA

ISBN: 978-0-9964610-0-9
First Edition

This book is available at quantity discounts for bulk purchases. For information please visit kristenrampe.com.

Dedicated to all CPAs
who love to laugh.

BOOK SELECTION PROCESS

A Flowchart Introduction

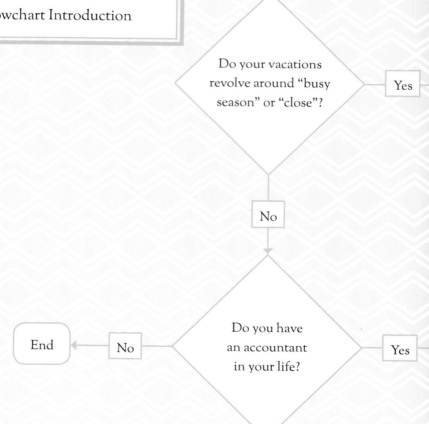

Do your vacations revolve around "busy season" or "close"?

Yes

No

Do you have an accountant in your life?

Yes

No

End

Remember when you started studying accounting because you "liked math"? Then you realized one day, "This isn't about math!"

And now you work tirelessly (or half asleep), meeting your client's needs, or your CPA's requests. And sometimes it isn't the beautiful, orderly world your college advisor promised you. Clients get angry. CPAs get disorganized. Everyone loves to blame the PCAOB or the IRS.

But what if that all went away? What if your dreams of seamless projects, short request lists, undisputed fees and people who bring you good food came true?

Read on...

You might think accountants are people who like pocket protectors, multiple monitors and numbers that match. But did you know that we have dreams too? Dreams of respect, reward for hard work, and quality office supplies?

All day, accountants are working hard to save you money, cost you money and produce financial data free from material error. If you want to give back and put a smile on your accountant's face, this book should do the trick.

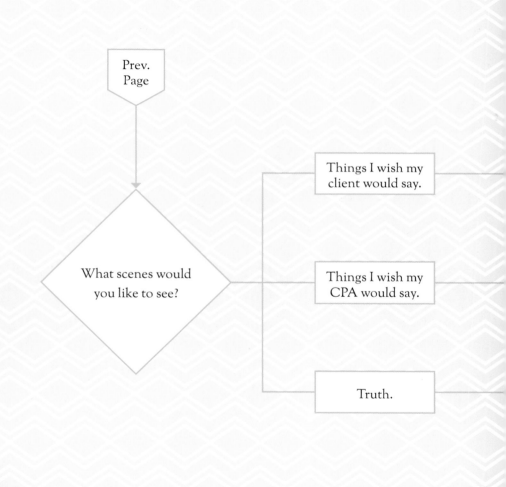

Prev.
Page

What scenes would
you like to see?

Things I wish my
client would say.

Things I wish my
CPA would say.

Truth.

CONTENTS

PART 1: CPA DREAMS

"So there I was, and you'll never believe what my client said…"

WOW, GREAT RATES!

Who knew accounting fees could be so reasonable?

*Do you mind if
I give you everything*
A WEEK EARLY?

*The CFO thought
your team would
prefer working in his
corner office over*
**SHARING THOSE
TWO CUBICLES.**

I KNOW YOU DON'T HAVE A DRAFT OF THE RETURN READY.

I just wanted to drop off some of our fresh flowers for you guys.

Even though we use ShadyBooks,
I wouldn't dream of making
a prior period entry.

ACCOUNTING NEWS

CPA Appreciation Week Set for May 3rd

HOLLYWOOD, CA – The Society of CPA Firm Clients has chosen the venue and activities for next year's CPA Appreciation Week.

The event will take place in Hollywood, and plans to feature wax models of the Top 100 CPAs, software vendor booths dedicated to taking suggestions for new enhancements, an intern dunk tank, and free alcohol.

Several movie stars will also be on hand to honor the hard working accountants, as the event is timed to coincide with the opening of the long-anticipated remake of Office Space.

"There is not a lot of public praise and celebration for CPAs, and it's our goal to change that." said SCPAFC president Wanda McNally.

The Society of CPA Firm Clients is a national group, focused on improving the image and overall happiness of CPAs across the country. Tax deductible donations to their non-profit can be made online and will automatically notify your tax accountant.

This one even auto-corrects every time you transpose a number. Happy birthday!

I have a board meeting coming up **IN ABOUT TWO MONTHS,** *would you have time to prepare a status update for us?*

Ooops, my bad.
You did include the attachment
in a previous email.

I'm more than happy to get that data to you, **YOUR EFFICIENCY IS A TOP PRIORITY FOR OUR TEAM.**

NEW CLIENT ACCEPTANCE QUESTIONNAIRE

Company name:_____

Completed by:_____

1. Did your former CPA drop you as a client? ☐ Yes ☐ No

2. Have you ever paid a bill more than 60 days late? ☐ Yes ☐ No

3. Has anyone referred to you as: an asshole, a jerk, or "challenging"? ☐ Yes ☐ No

4. Do you have a history of changing jobs because you can't do the work, or don't get along with people? If yes, please explain: ☐ Yes ☐ No

5. Has the SEC sanctioned you or have you been subjected to court-ordered anger management classes? ☐ Yes ☐ No

6. Do you love the sound of deadlines whooshing by? ☐ Yes ☐ No

7. Can you perform basic arithmetic? ☐ Yes ☐ No

8. Do you have **ANY** hobbies? ☐ Yes ☐ No

FOR INTERNAL USE ONLY:

Accepted?	Reason:	
☐ Yes	☐ Would go out for a beer with them	☐ Would like to date them
	☐ Used to work for our firm	☐ Paid in full up front
☐ No	☐ Idiot	☐ Creeps me out
	☐ Used to work for competitor	☐ Totally unprepared for, or forgot about, our first meeting

We agree with all of these proposed adjustments. Thank you for helping keep us on the right track!

You need to do another inventory of our assets, don't you?

PART 2: CLIENT DELUSIONS

"And then my CPA said to me…"

I made sure the staff on your engagement are the same as last year, so we won't ask **ANY REPETITIVE QUESTIONS.**

I chose a career in accounting because **I LOVE WORKING WITH PEOPLE.**

This is the first, and last,
request list you'll receive from us.

*Ooops, **MY** bad.*
You did include the attachment
in a previous email.

I'm here to massage your numbers.

Our clients find this much easier than talking to us.

FREE
New Client Onboarding Gift!

CPA
REPELLANT

WHEN YOU NEED A LITTLE EXTRA TIME TO PREPARE.

51

It will only take me one day to draft financials for your five subsidiaries.

Your refund is $1,000,000!

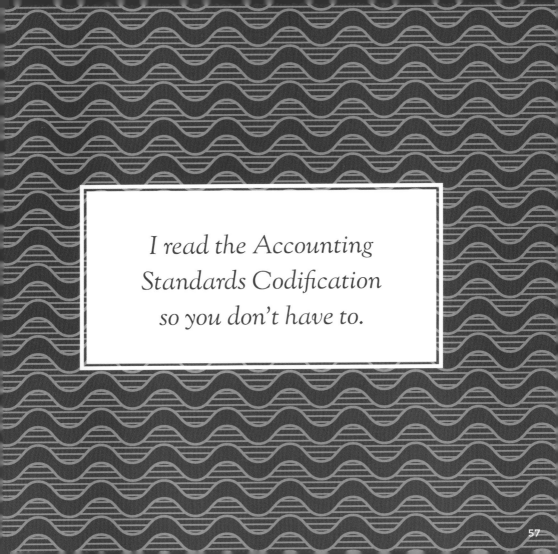

I read the Accounting
Standards Codification
so you don't have to.

You **ARE** *my only client.*

THIS DEPARTMENT
HAS WORKED

283 DAYS

WITHOUT A LOST
CLIENT DOCUMENT

THE BEST PREVIOUS
RECORD WAS

4 DAYS

DO YOUR PART!
HELP MAKE
A NEW RECORD

I hate deadlines anyway.

No evidence?
No problem.

I see some significant over-runs here. We'll have to write those off.

*We have no
additional questions.*

PART 3: NIGHTMARES & REALITIES

"What she said."

Did I send that message without the attachment?

You'll lead the inventory in the HazMat location.

Kevin is your new senior.
He's one of our best!

ACCOUNTING NEWS

IRS to Set Mileage Reimbursement Rates Each Day

WASHINGTON, DC – In order to keep up with fluctuating oil and gas prices, the IRS announced today that it will now set mileage reimbursement rates on a daily basis.

"Gas stations change their prices pretty much every day, why shouldn't we?" said senior IRS staffer Angela Ford. Citing an interest in pin-point accurate financial data, rather than ease of use, Ms. Ford expressed that the IRS is pleased to further their mission through this change.

The new policy will go into effect tomorrow requiring updates to mileage tracking systems each day until software companies design something more efficient, in about two years.

Abe founded our Work-Life Integration initiative.

You did **WHAT**
at the holiday party?!

Annual Meeting: Quiz Show Categories

Keystrokes	Acronyms	Famous CPAs	"Appears Reasonable"	Vacations I Haven't Taken	Scope Creep Tactics
200	**200**	**200**	**200**	**200**	**200**
400	**400**	**400**	**400**	**400**	**400**
600	**600**	**#DIV/0!**	**600**	**600**	**600**
800	**800**	**#DIV/0!**	**800**	**800**	**800**
1000	**1000**	**#DIV/0!**	**1000**	**1000**	**1000**

You mean this stuff
has to reconcile?

Can I have your fax number?

I'm sorry, ma'am,
I can't let you through.
**YOUR COMPANY'S
POLICY REQUIRES YOU
TO TAKE YOUR LAPTOP
ON VACATION.**

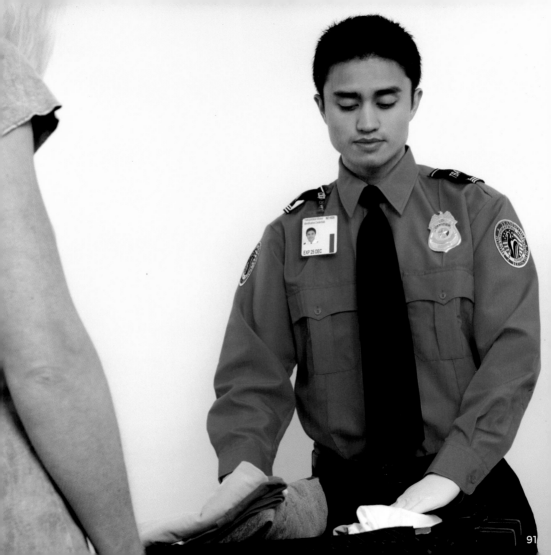

WANT MORE?

View outtakes or download your very own copy of the Client Acceptance Questionnaire at: kristenrampe.com/outtakes

ACKNOWLEDGEMENTS

CONTRIBUTORS AND REVIEWERS

Thank you for taking time out of your busy schedule to give me ideas, review comments and honest feedback to ensure I met standards of quality we are all accustomed to:

Alexis Claypool, Natasha Castelli, Melanie Kidder, Dan Rasmussen, Claudette MacMillan, Alita Eaton, Adam Blitz, Gaea Dennis, Jonathan Willyerd, Beckie Reilly, Tarryn Donahue, Bryan Coleman, Tom Kiley, Ralph Nach, Jessica Sacchetti, Joelle Shehadi, Dana Rudd, and Jason Williams.

PHOTO CREDITS

Thank you to the photographers and models whose great work and perfect expressions we found at iStockPhotography. A list of credits is available on our website at kristenrampe.com/book.

TYPOGRAPHY

Monserrat and Sorts Mill Goudy

SPECIAL THANKS

To my editor, Caleb, for signing up for this project without hesitation. Your appreciations and exercises perfected this book, gave me the courage to leave some professionalism behind, and gave readers far more to laugh about.

To my designer, Lauren, for an incredible array of talents that took this project from a simple document to an aesthetic masterpiece.

To my husband, Matt, for encouraging me to get this idea off the ground and reviewing it along the way. Without your support, I'd still be saying "I should write a book like this."

To the all-star GBC group (you know who you are) and extended family at Frank, Rimerman. I learned so much from all of you, and am grateful you appreciated my occasional pranks.